McFadden's Cold War

Cold War Steve

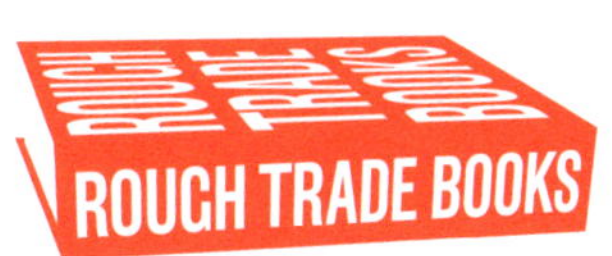

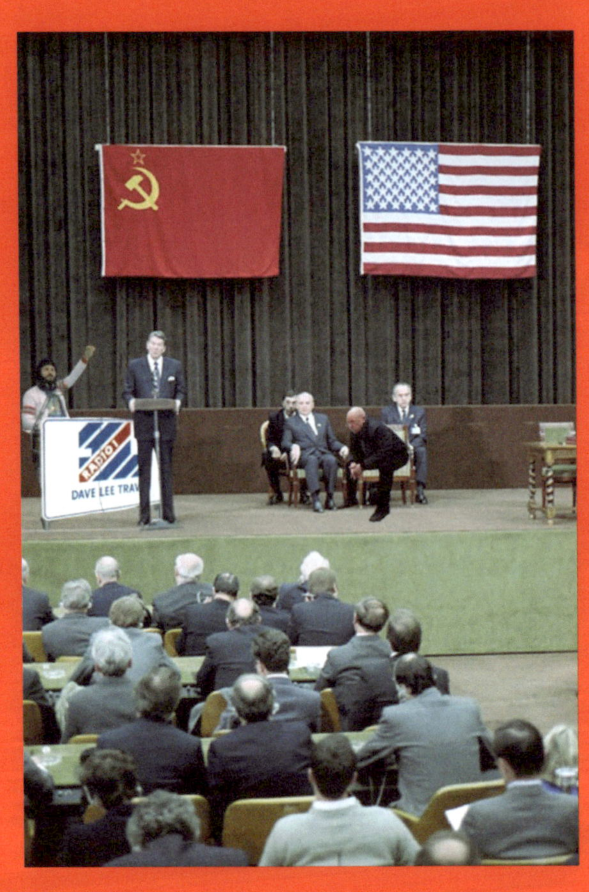
RADIO 1
DAVE LEE TRAV

Introduction

There was something quite refreshing seeing these early numbers again; stripped back, lo-fi, DIY, skiffle in a loft with washboards and tea-chests. Cut'n'paste, created in minutes, with the sole purpose of trying to make people laugh. Following a particularly dark period in my life, the joy and renewed focus I got from making these pictures certainly saved me.

Back when the 'Cold War' in Cold War Steve was a specific reference, I wasn't encumbered with concerns about image resolution and what have you. It was Steve McFadden (as Phil Mitchell in *Eastenders*) placed into a famous Cold War scene. A joke of incongruity—married with my fascination of the history of the Soviet Union and the Cold War—that I ran with for as long as I could.

The gradual introduction of other backdrops and characters, pieces becoming more satirical and taking much longer to produce, would come later. I was really thrilled therefore, to be able to present these 'early Peel Sessions' as a reminder, for myself more than anything, of where it all began. In those pre-referendum days of yore.

— *Christopher Spencer*

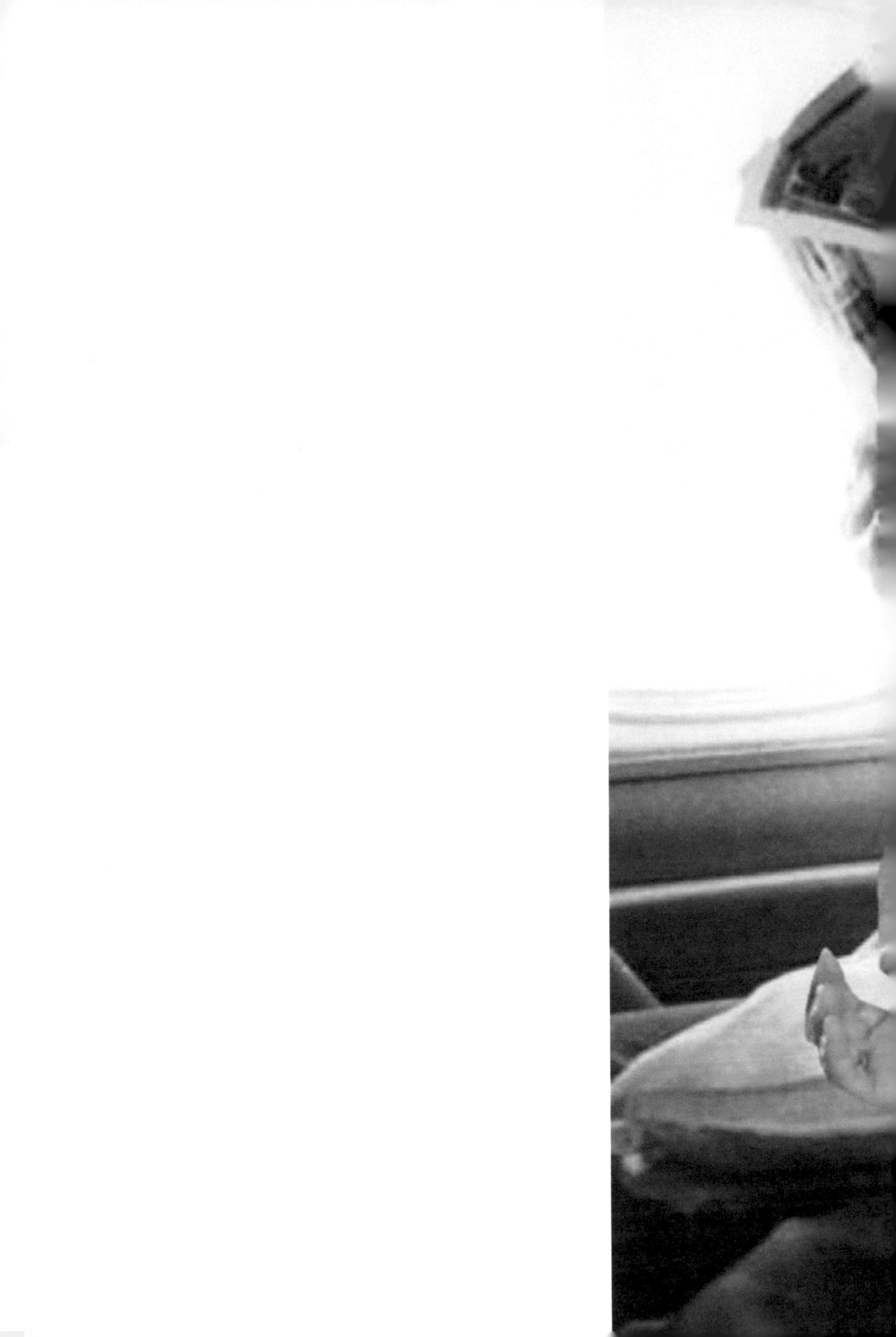

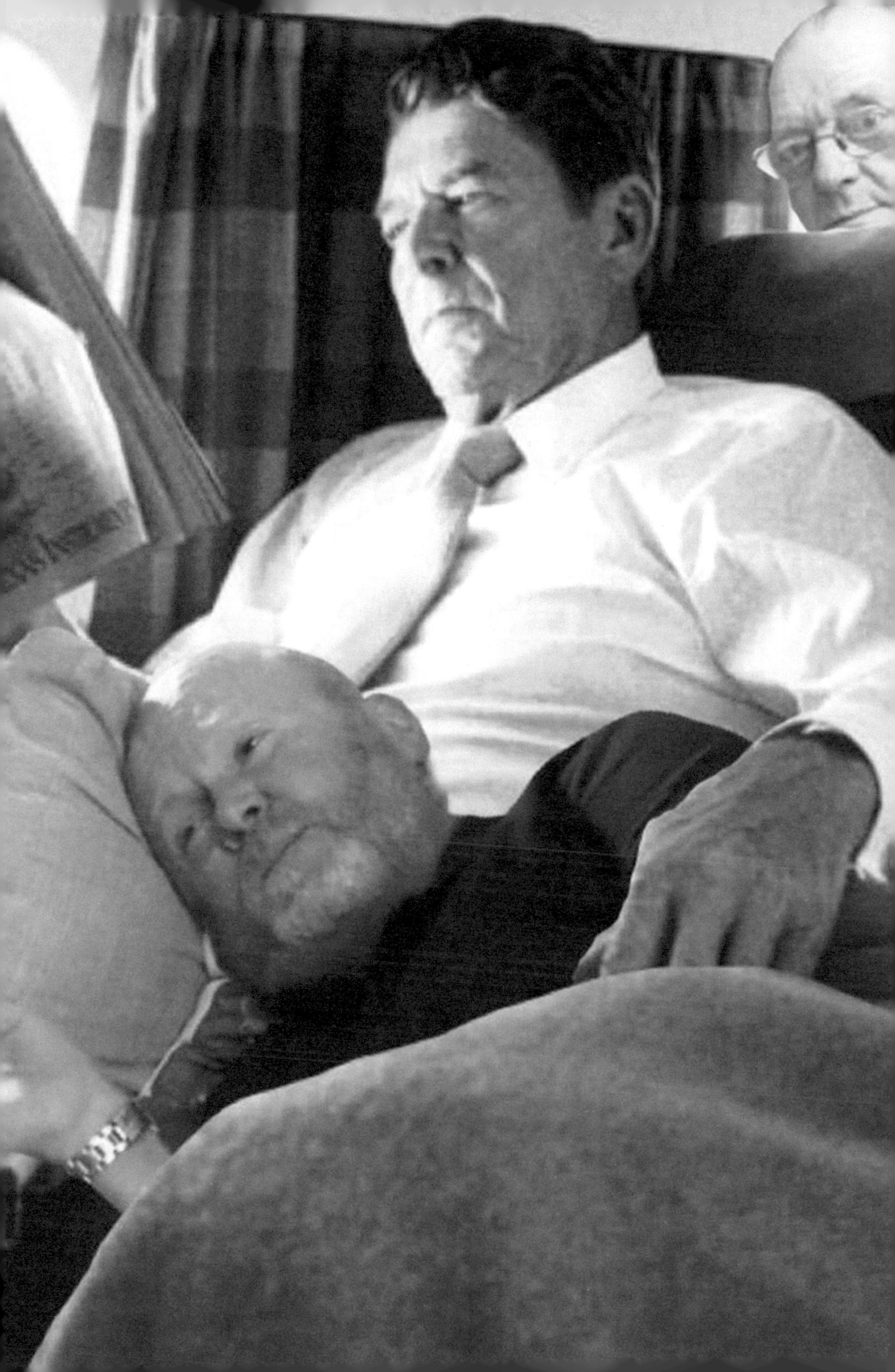

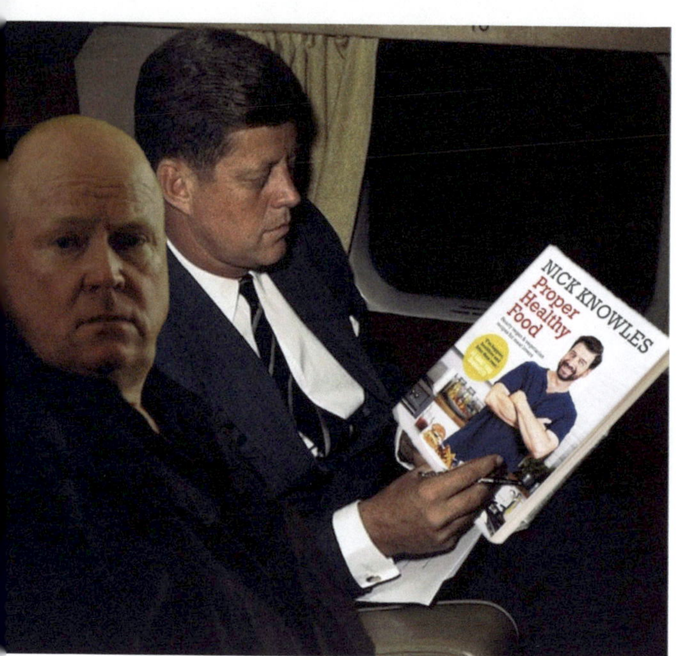
NICK KNOWLES
Proper
Healthy
Food

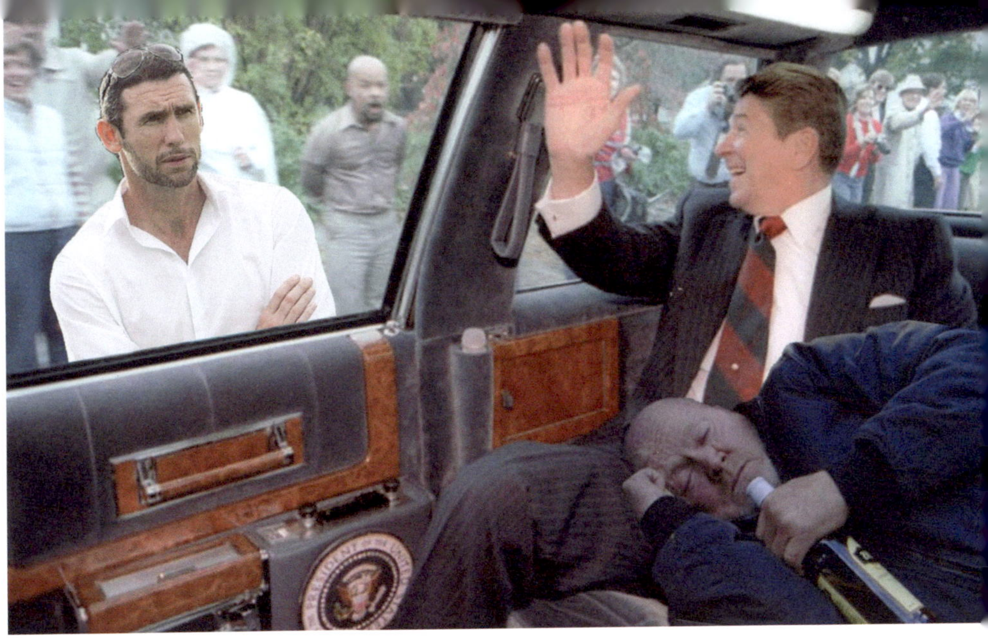

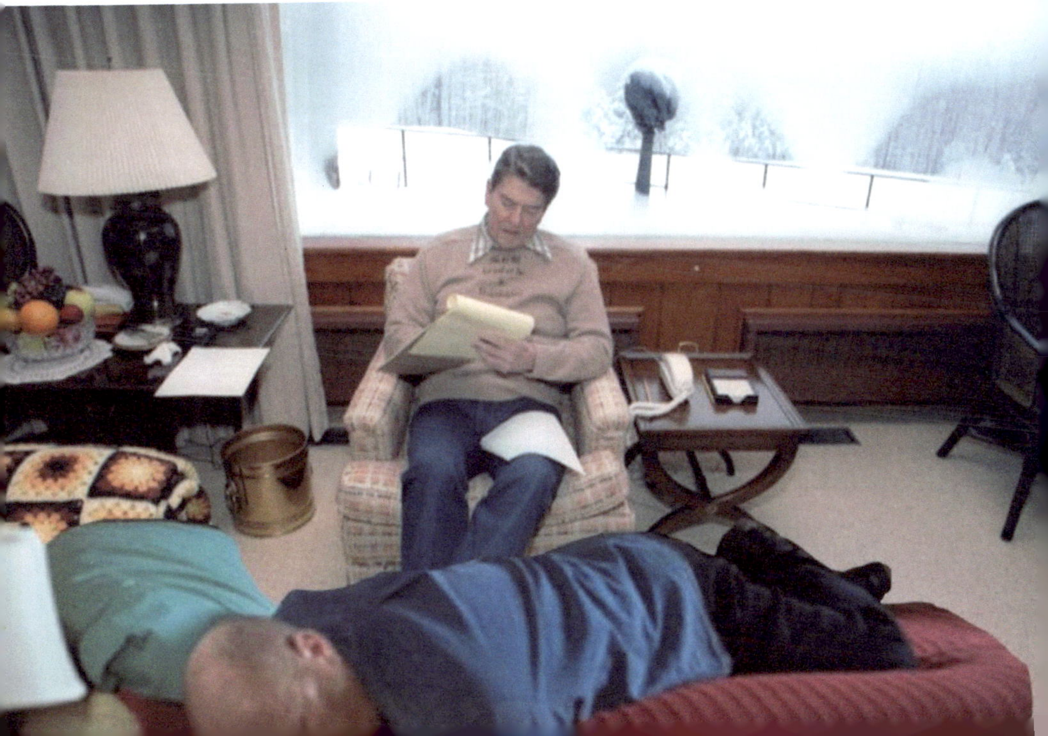

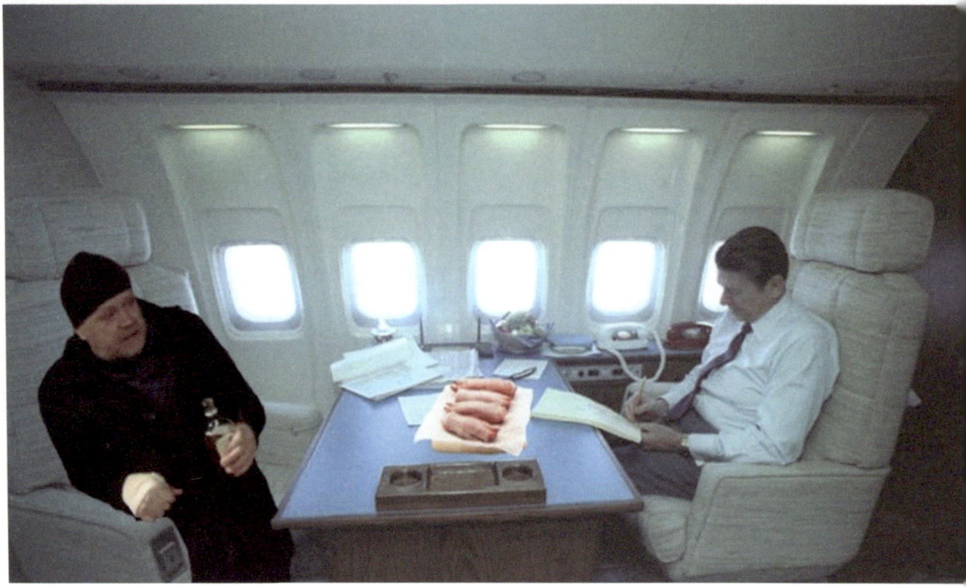

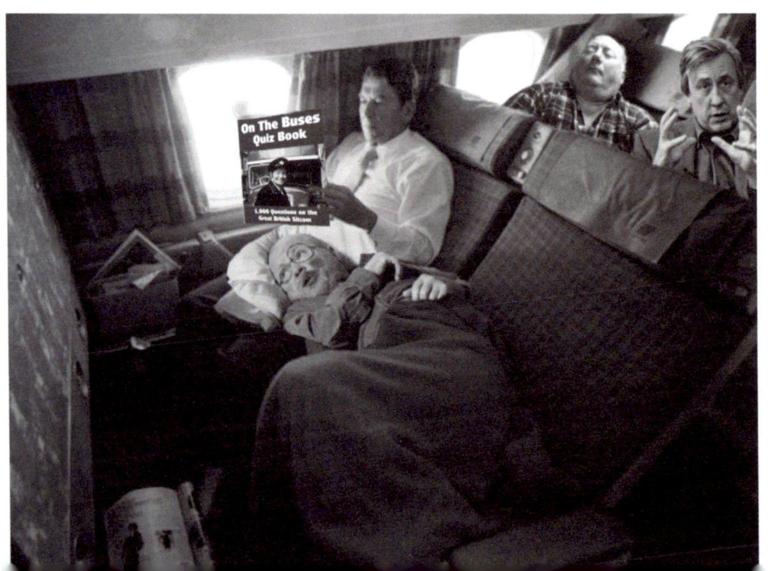
On The Buses
Quiz Book
1,000 Questions on the
Great British Sitcom

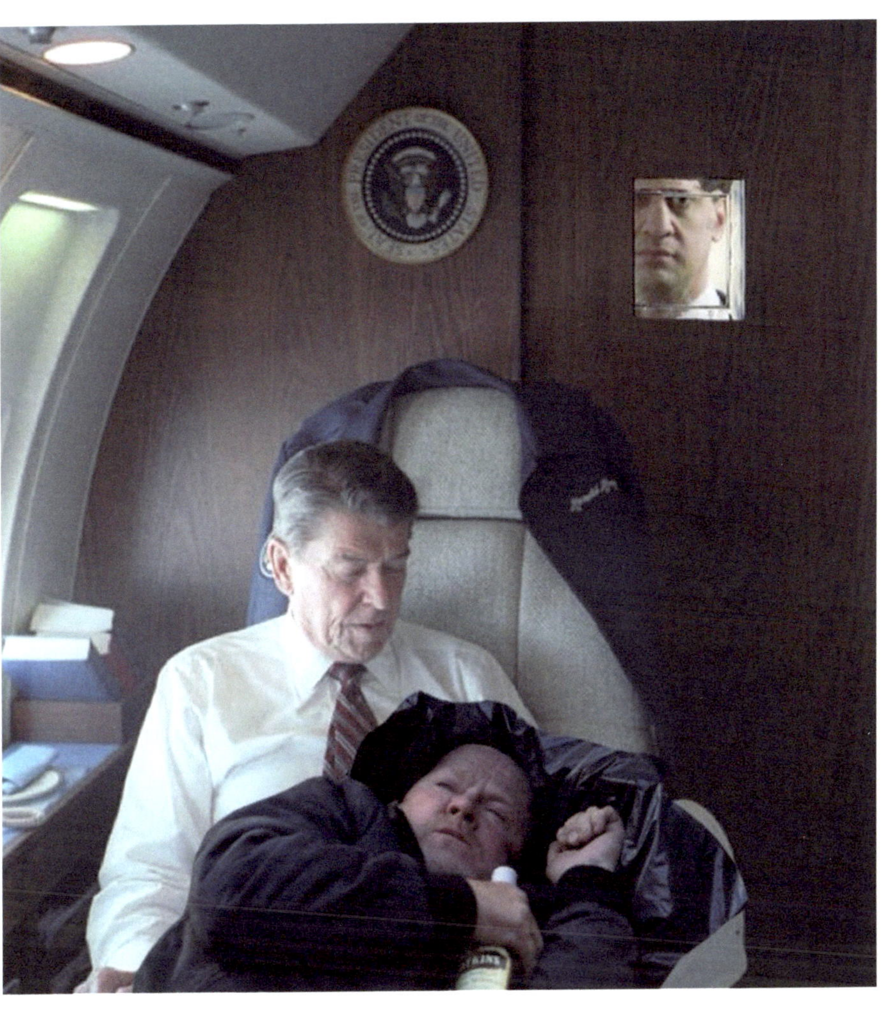

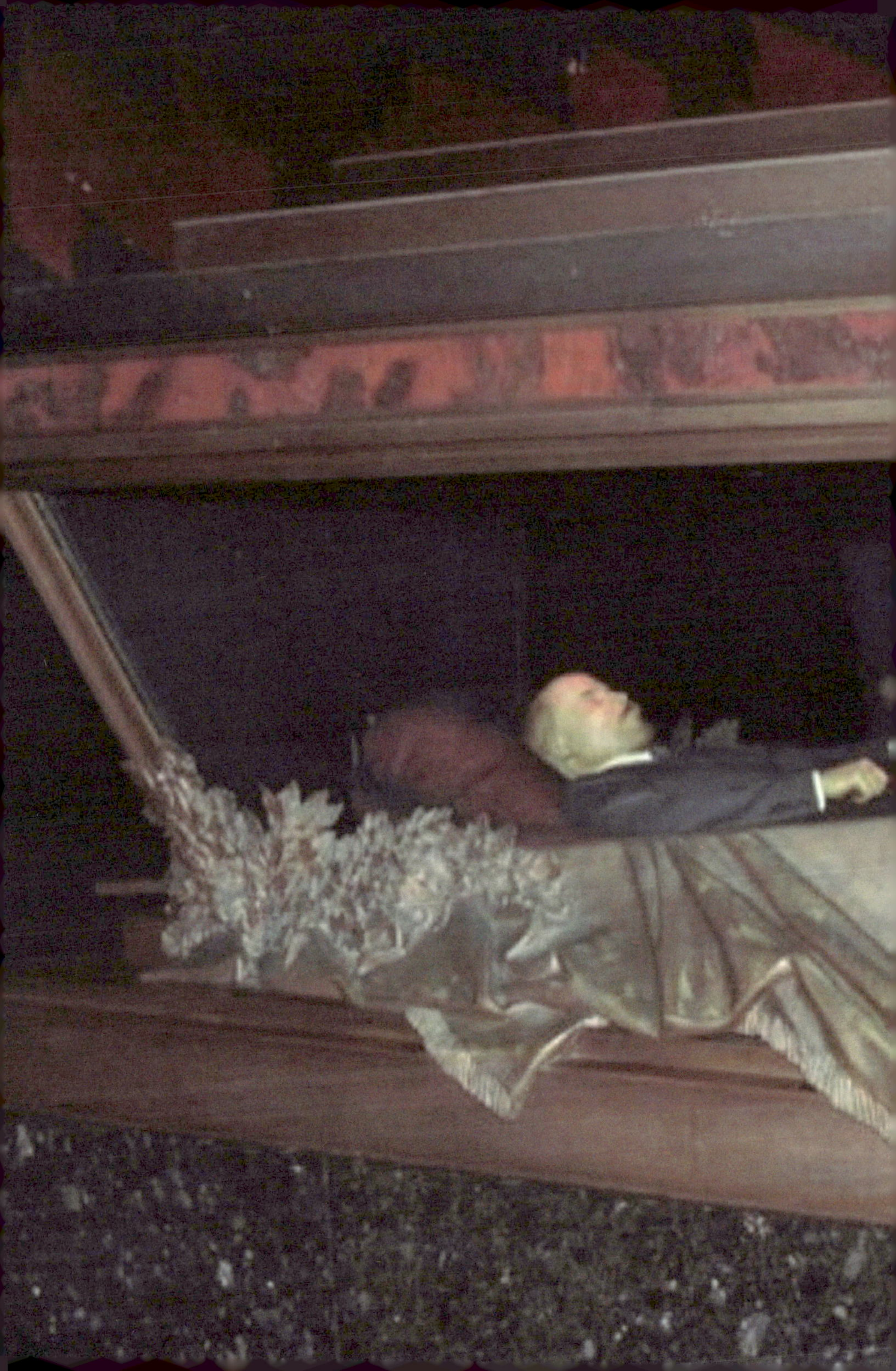

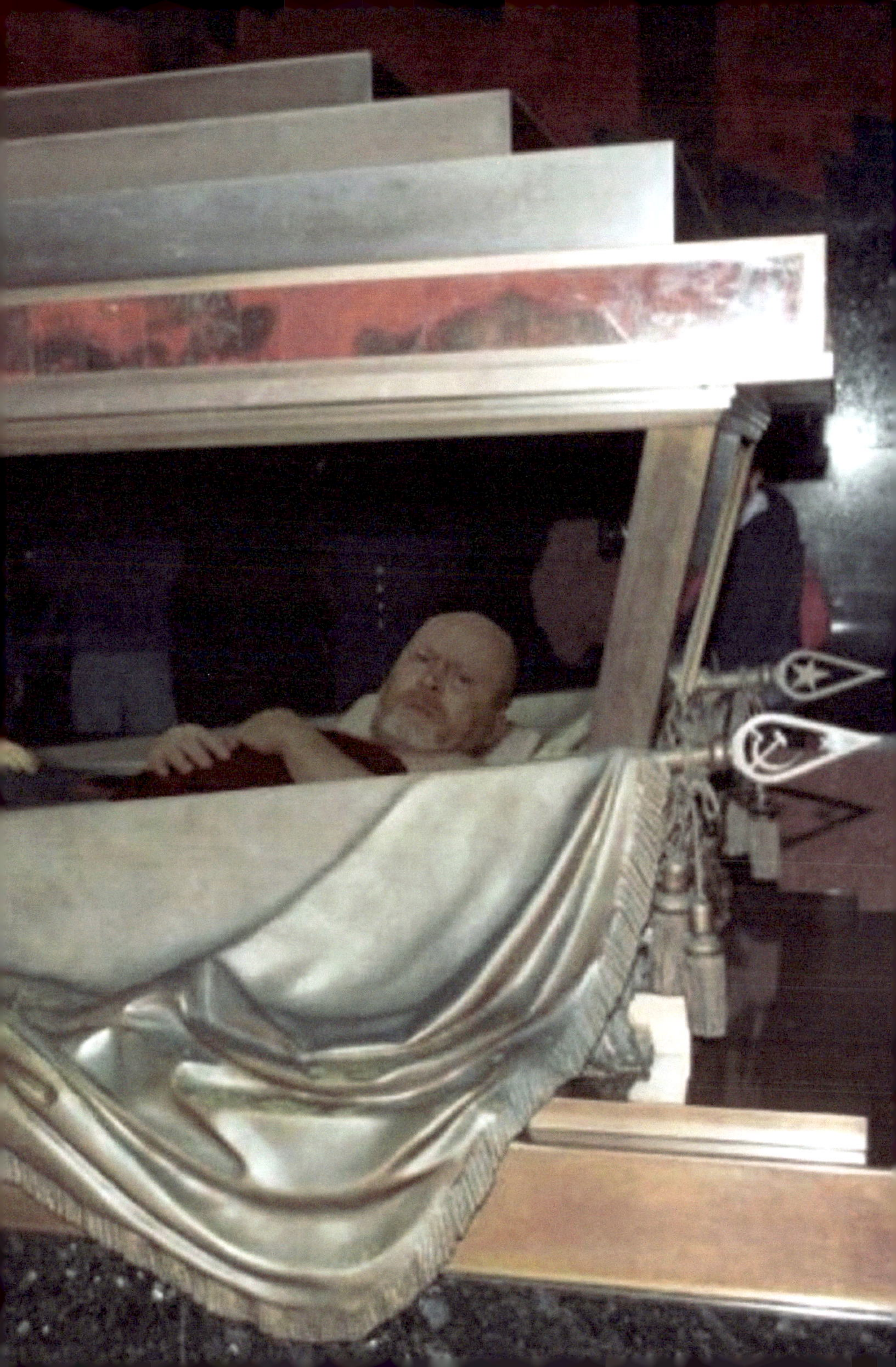

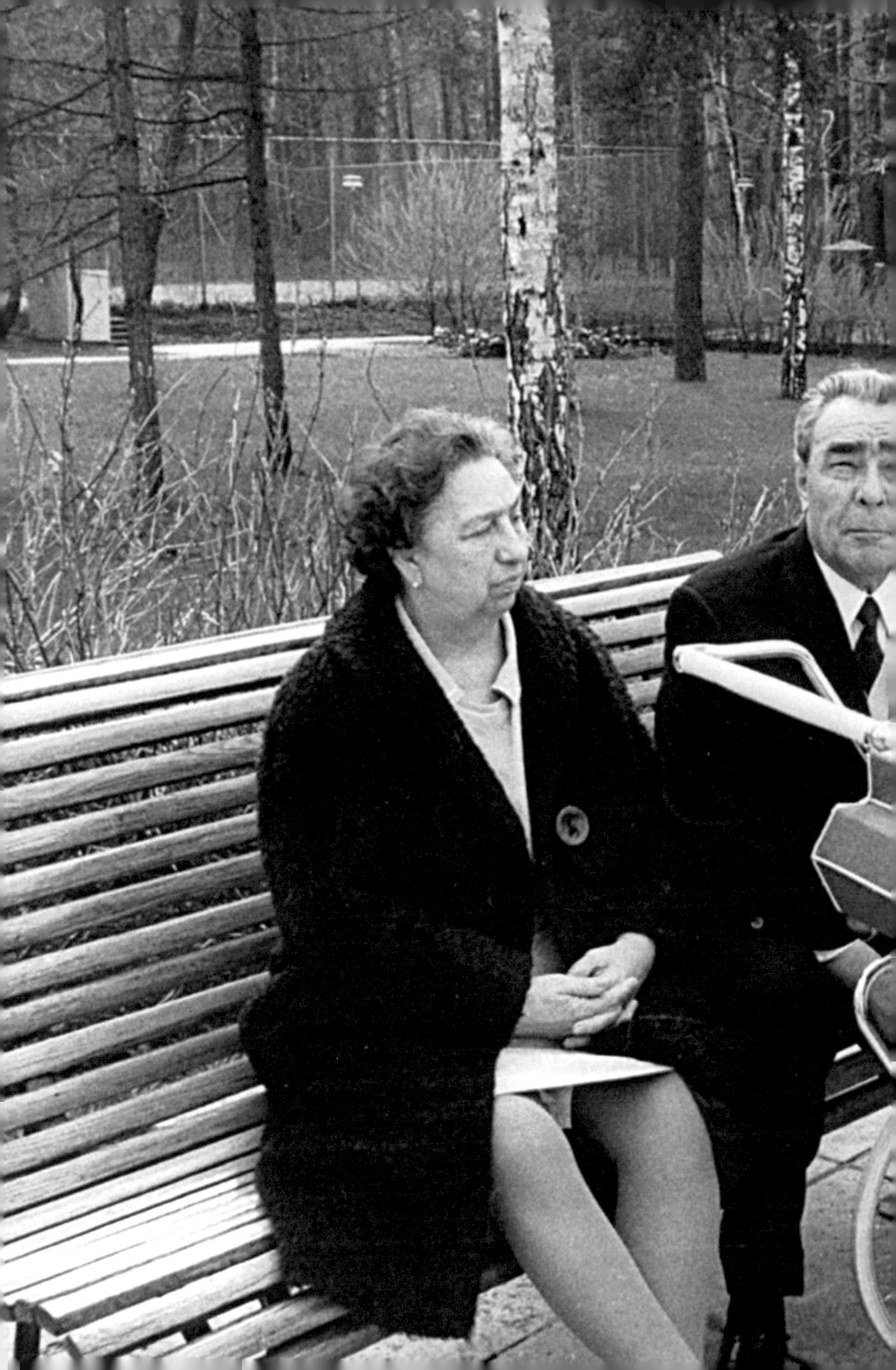

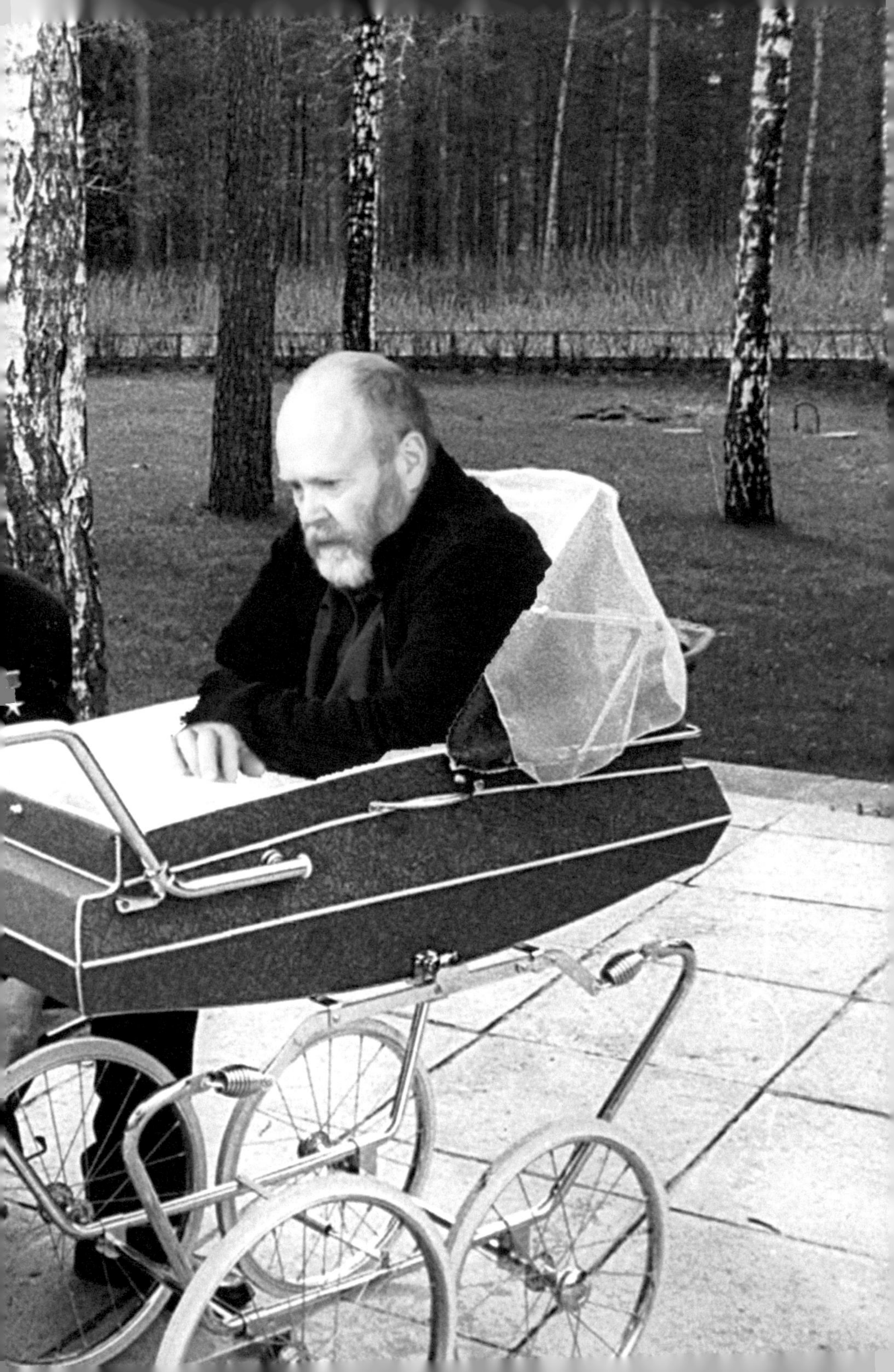

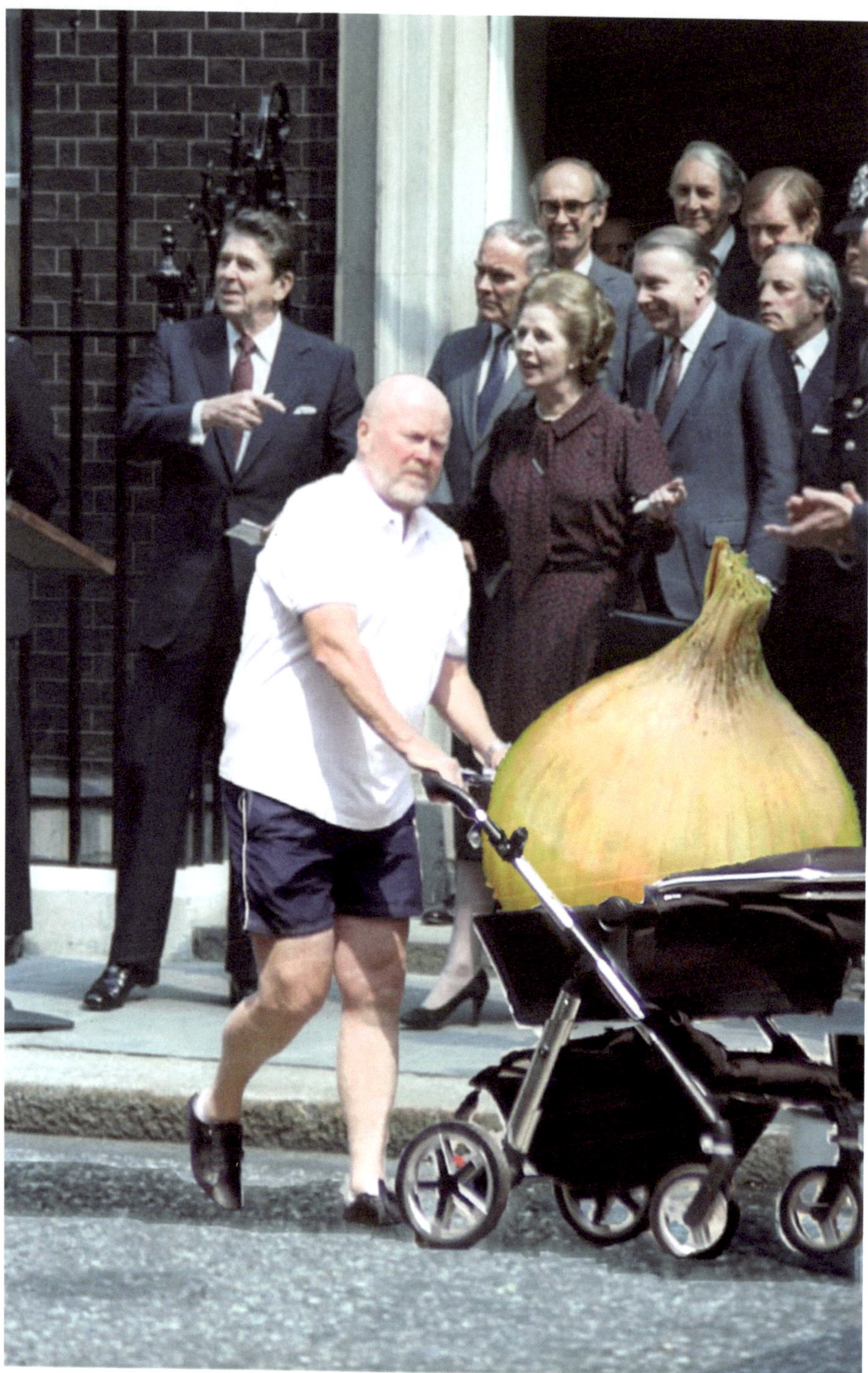

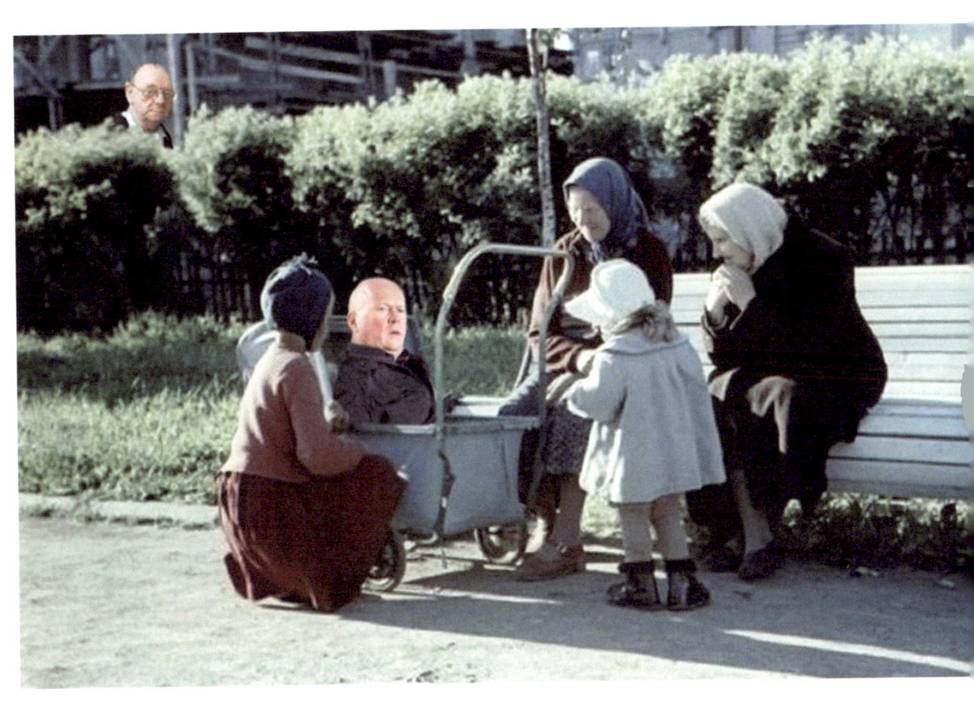

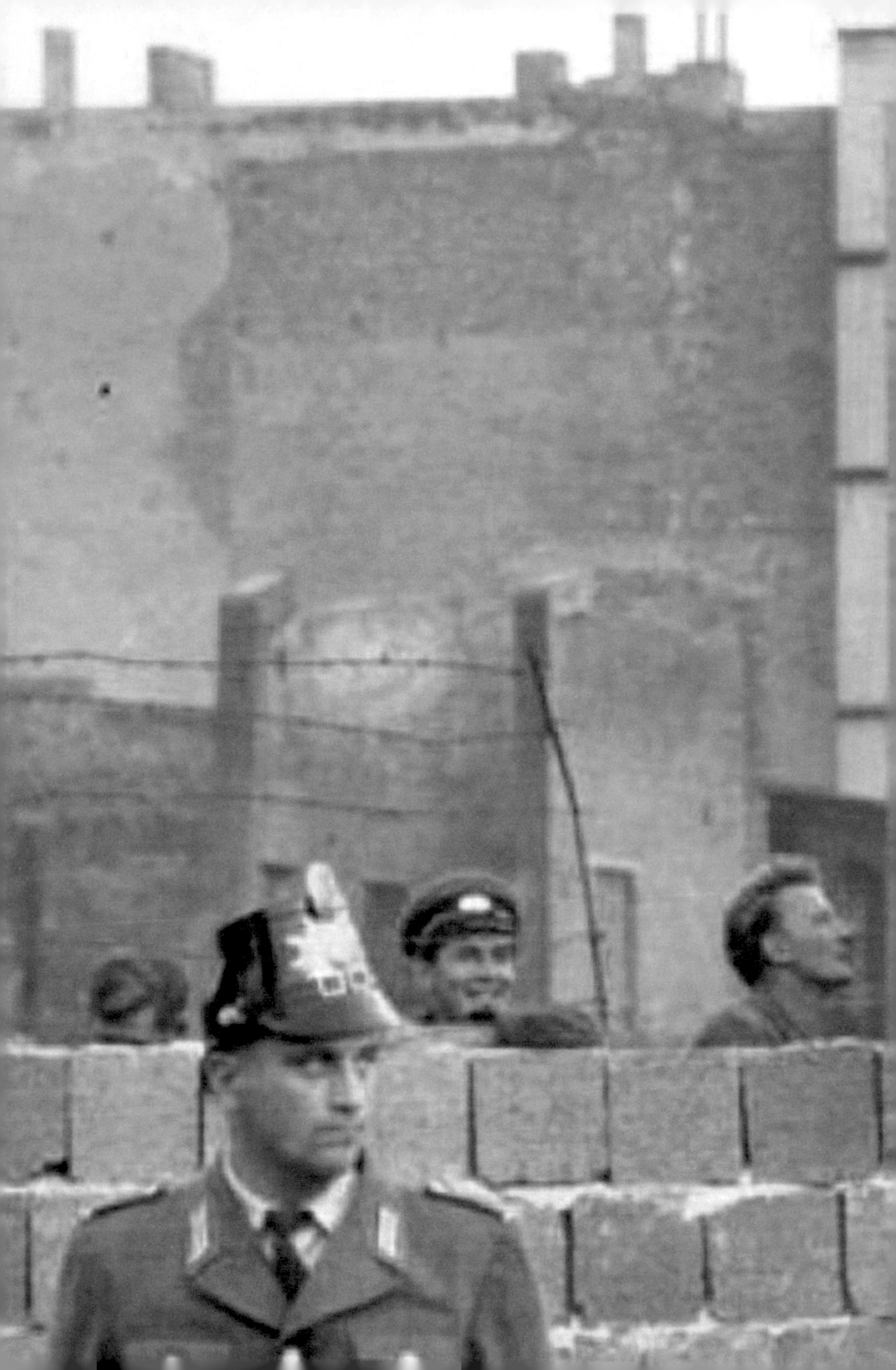

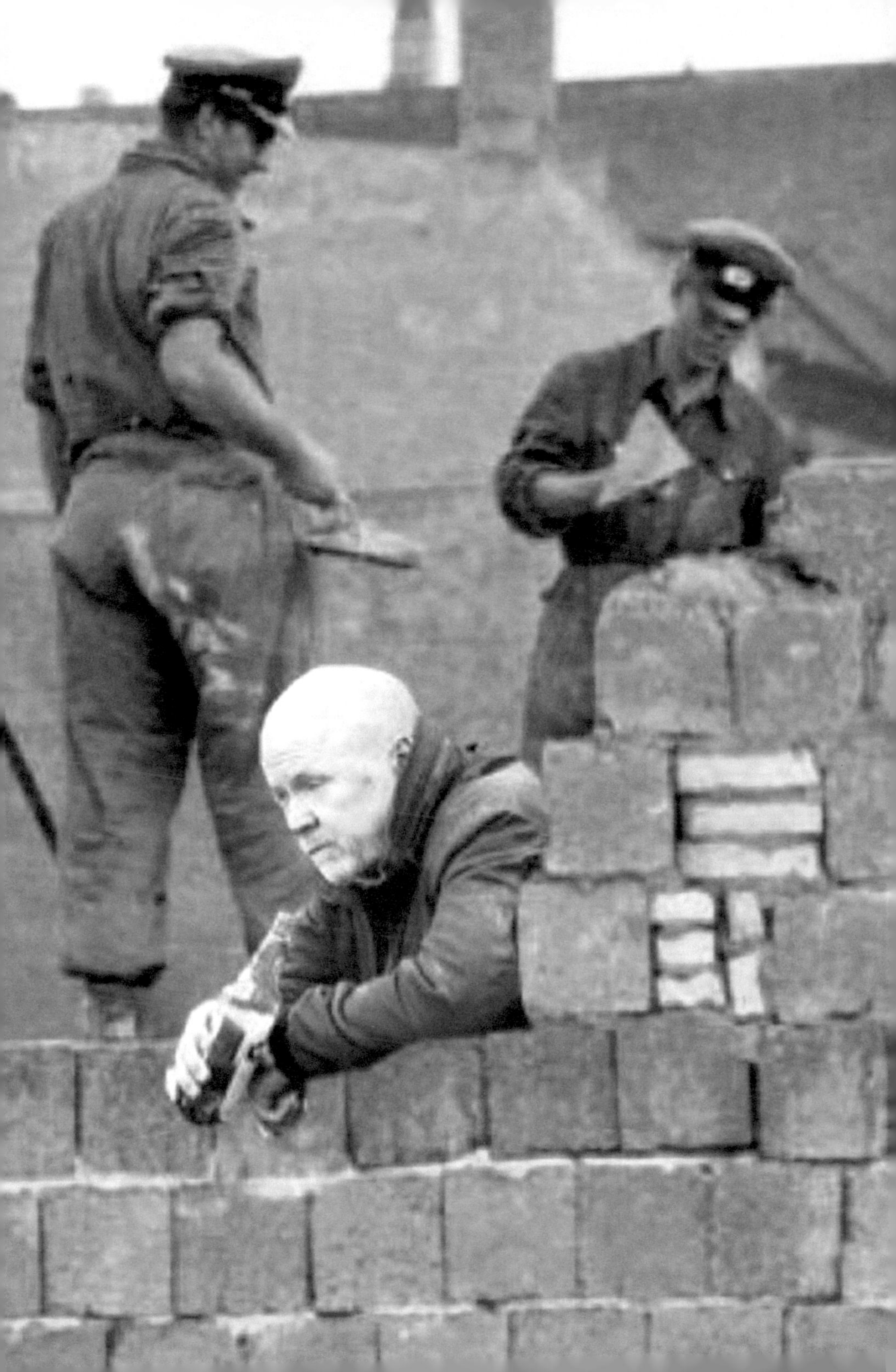

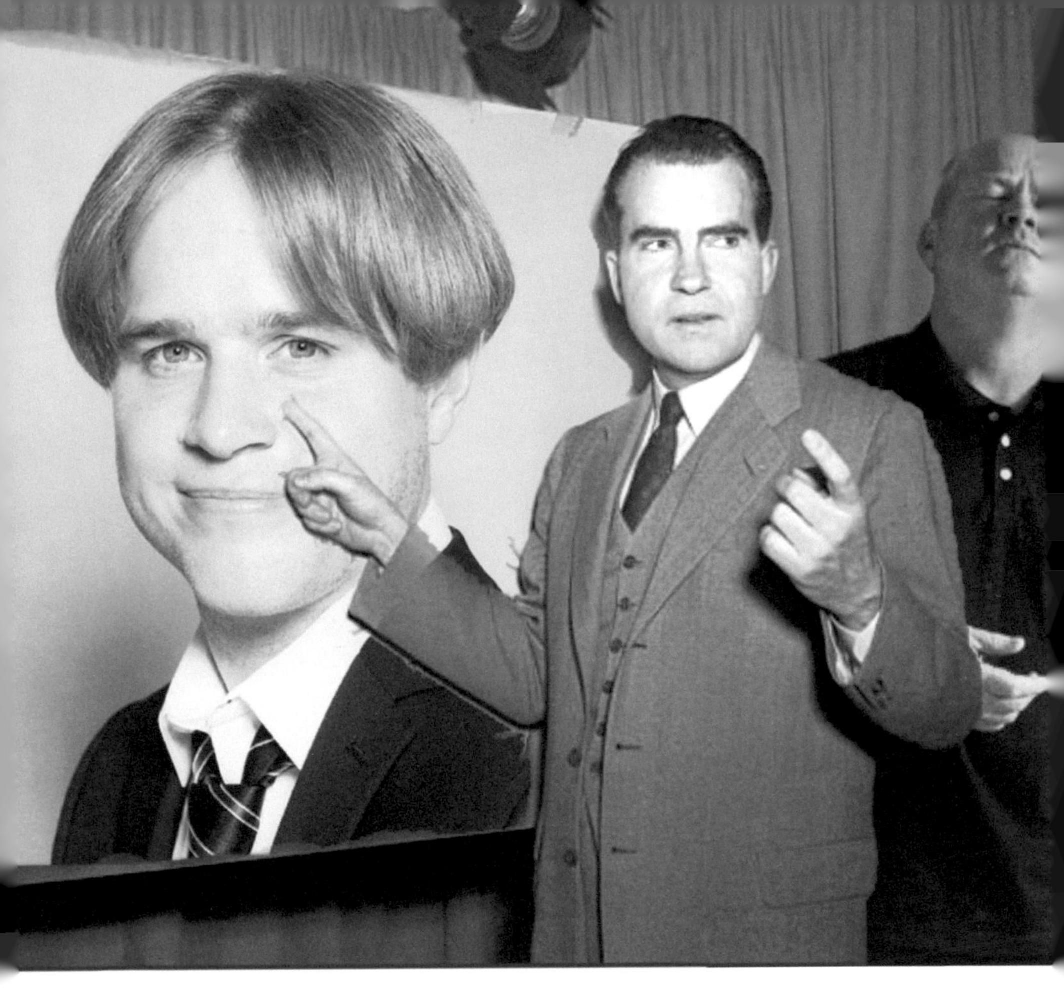

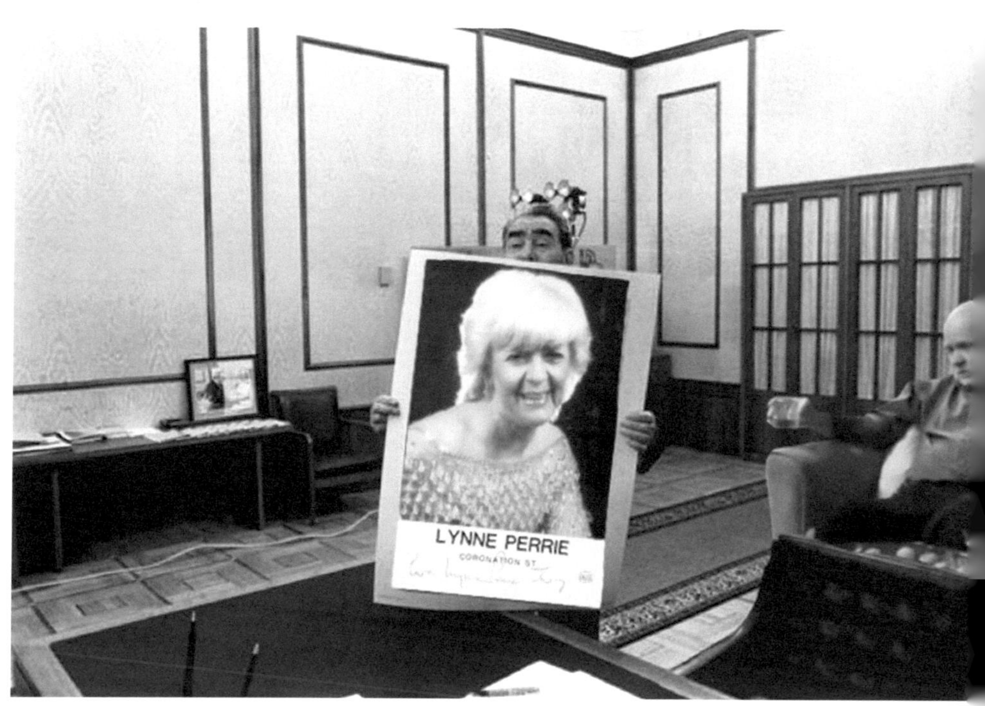
LYNNE PERRIE
CORONATION ST.

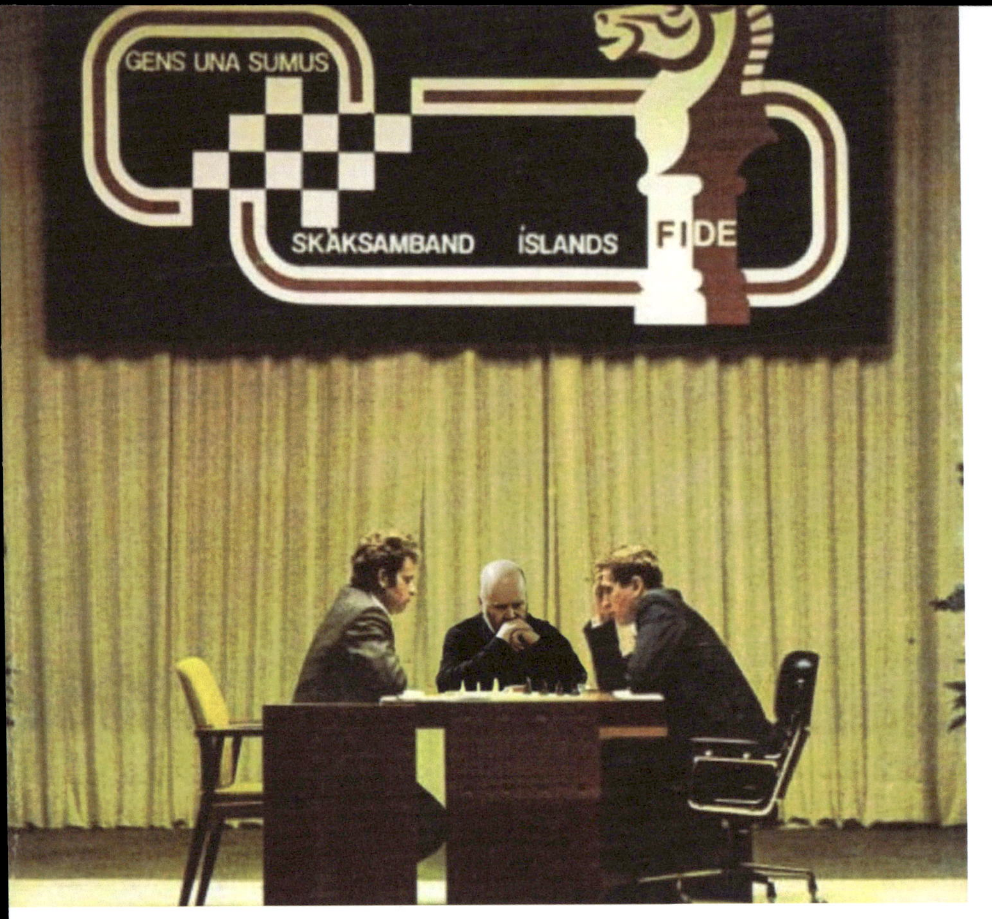
GENS UNA SUMUS
SKÁKSAMBAND ÍSLANDS
FIDE

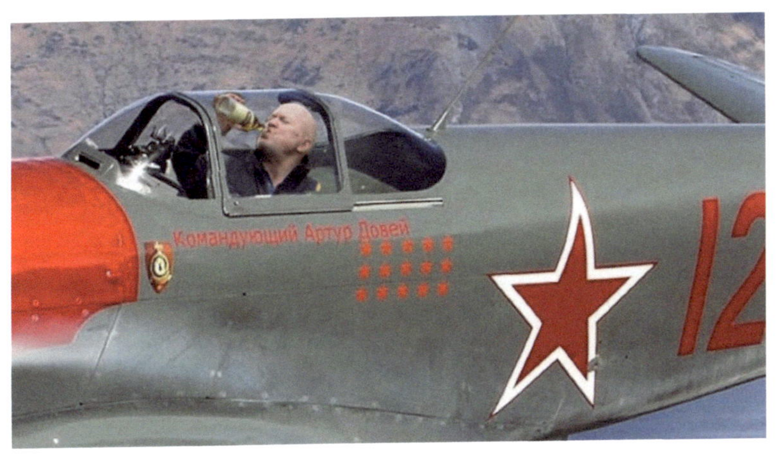
Командующий Артур Довей
12

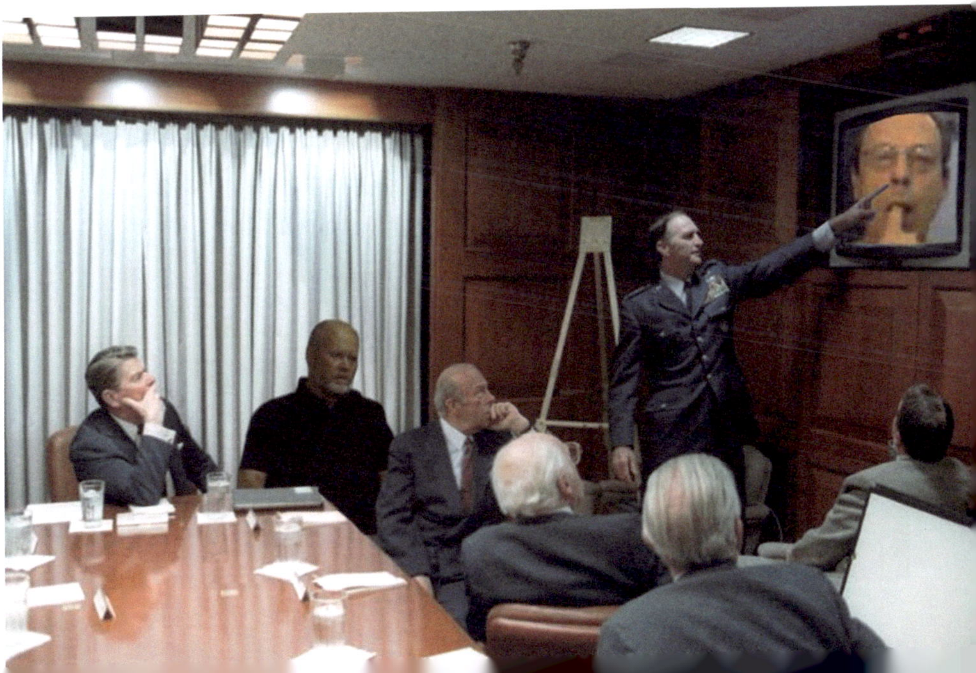

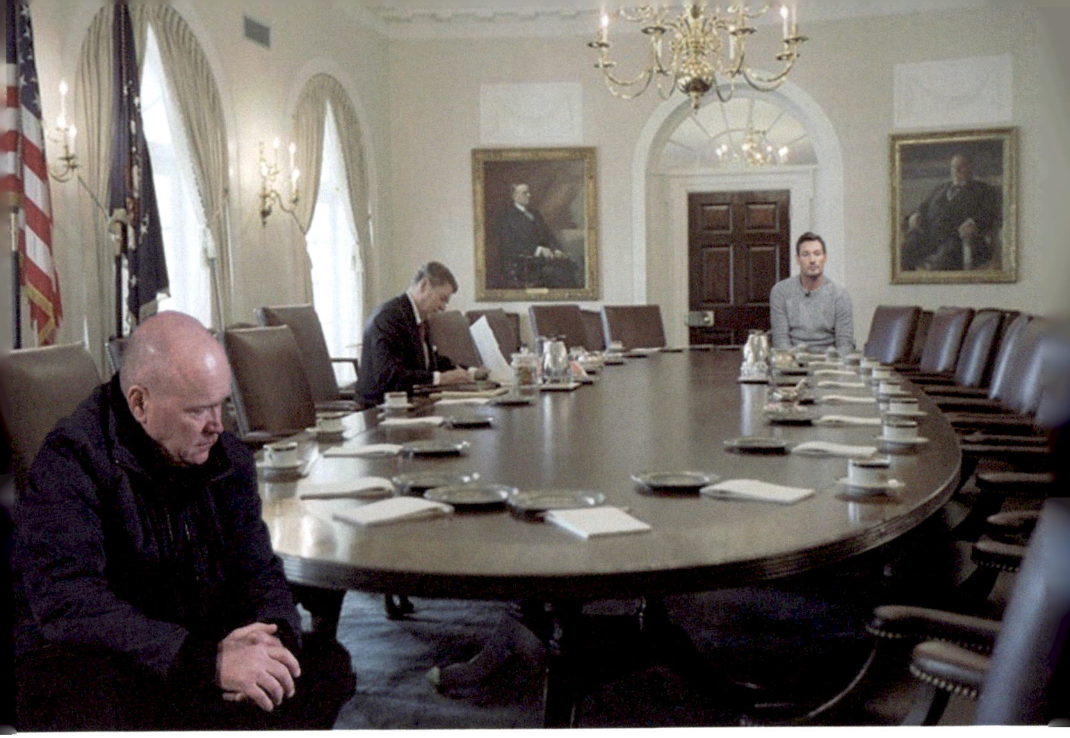

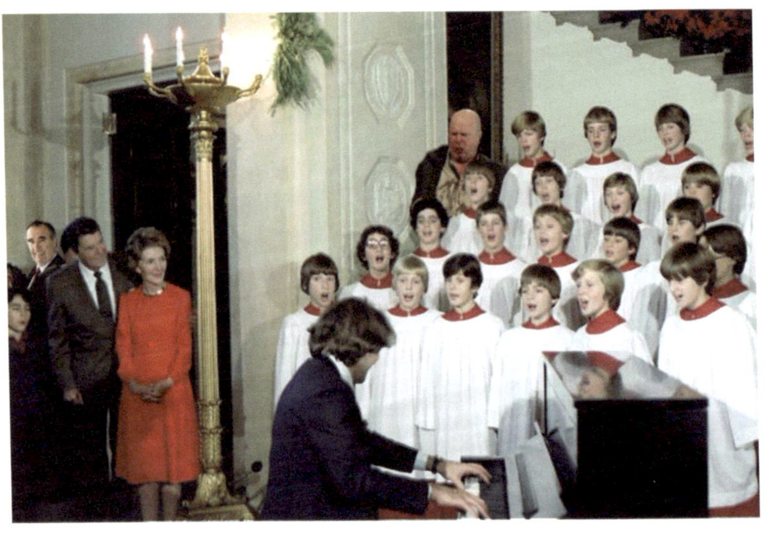

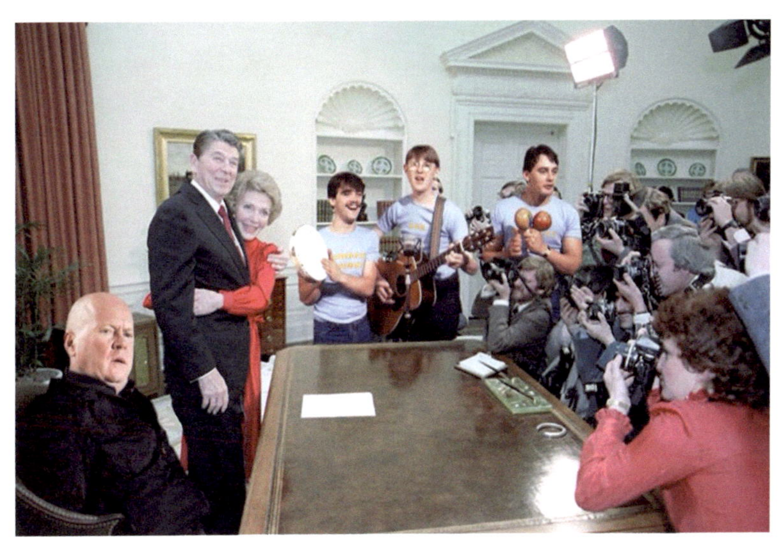

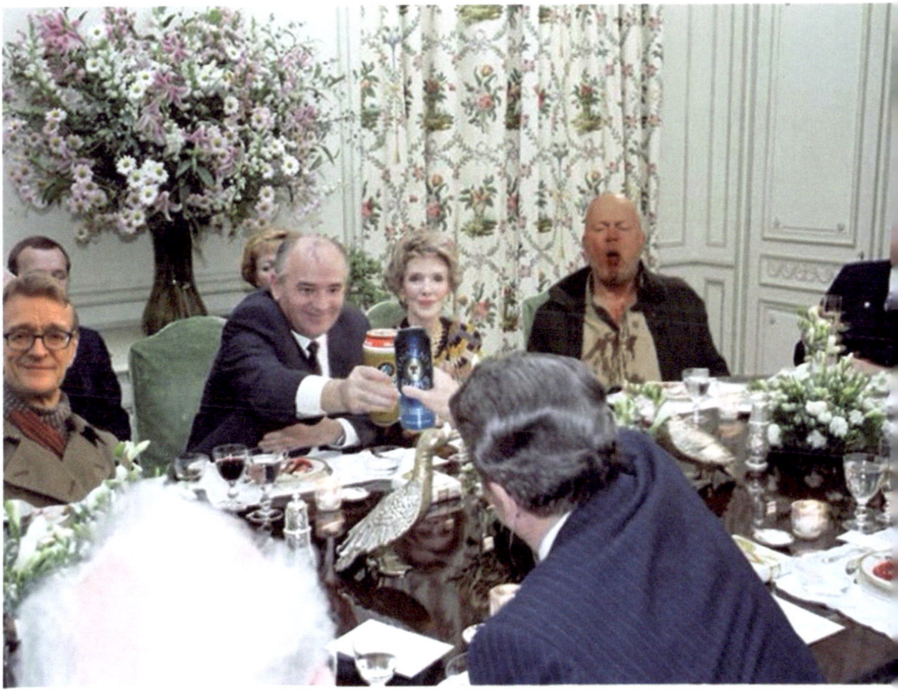

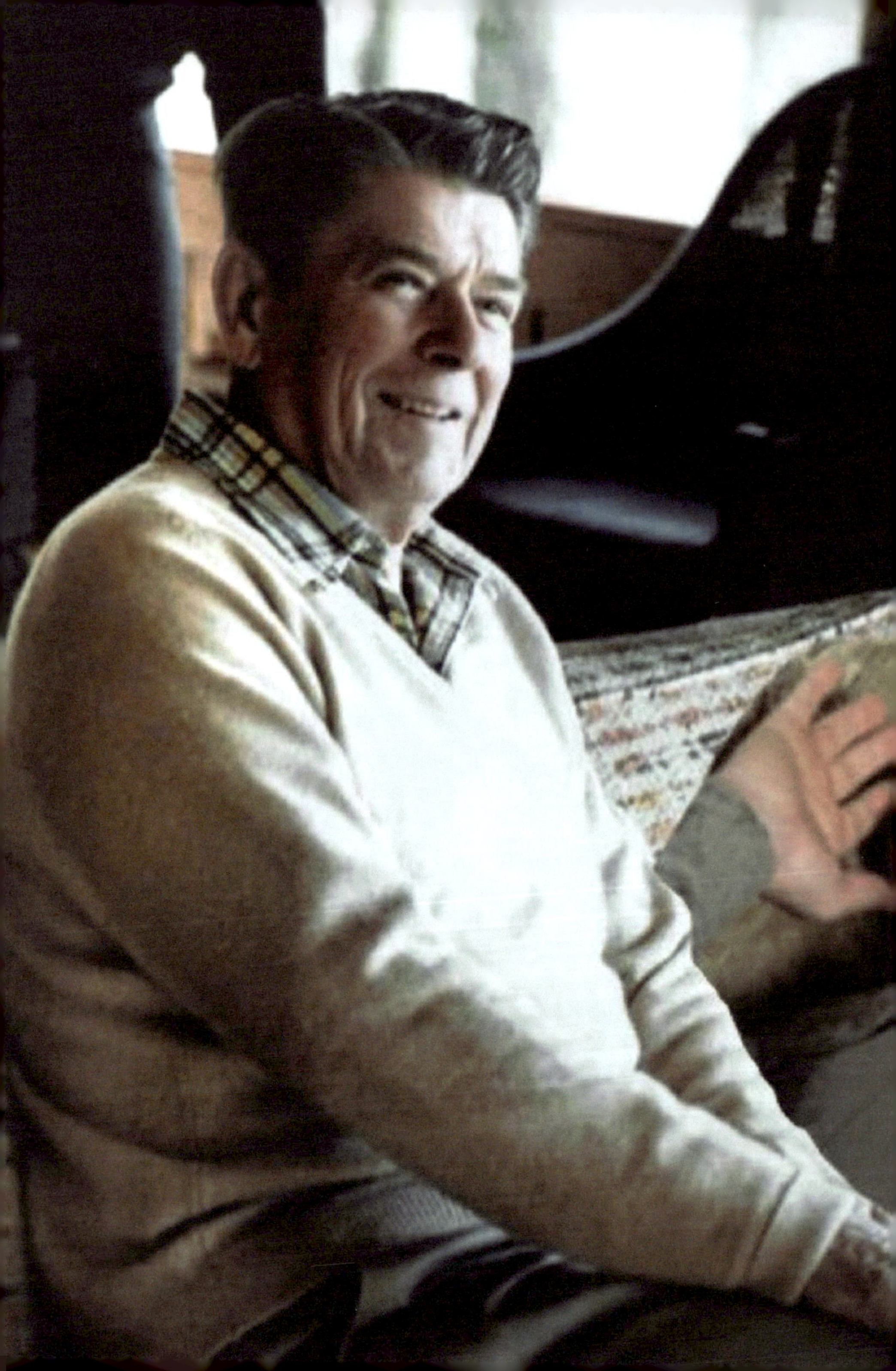

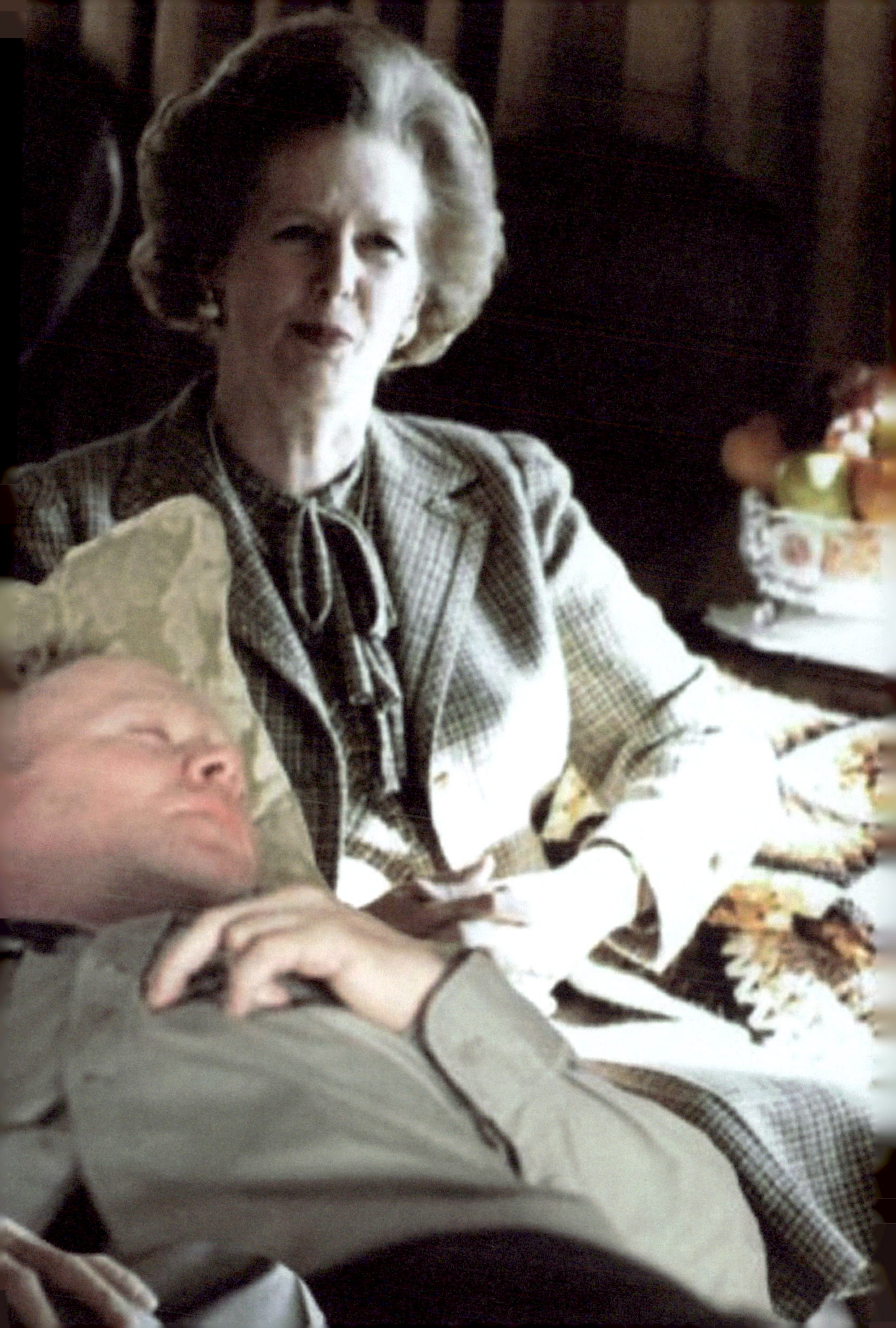

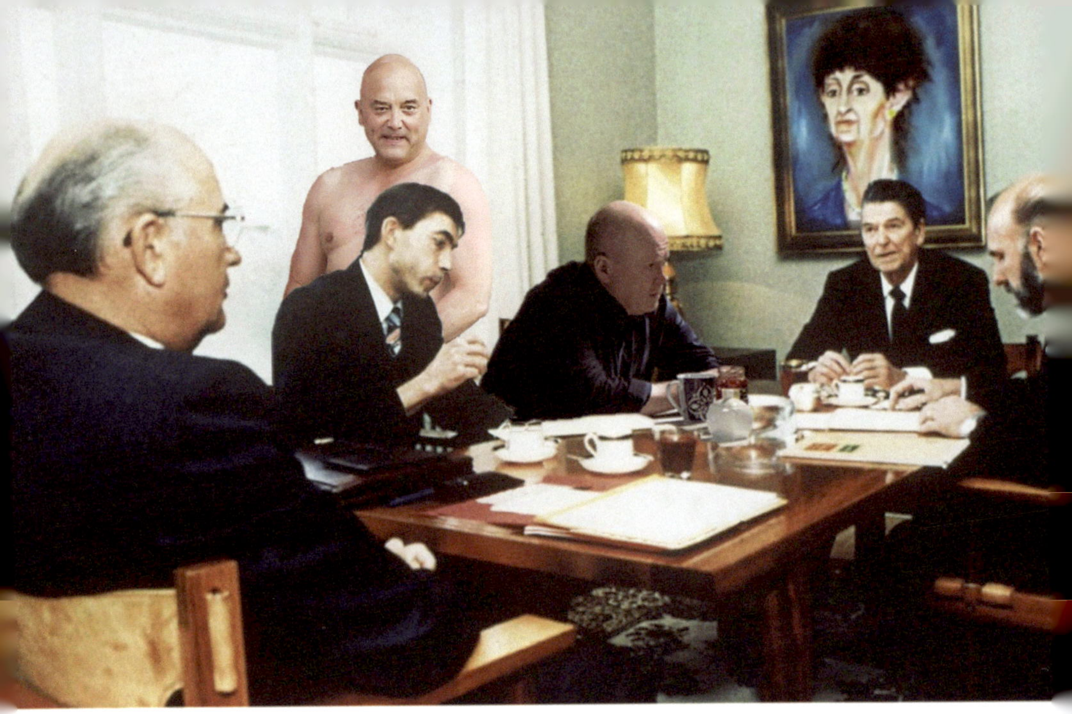

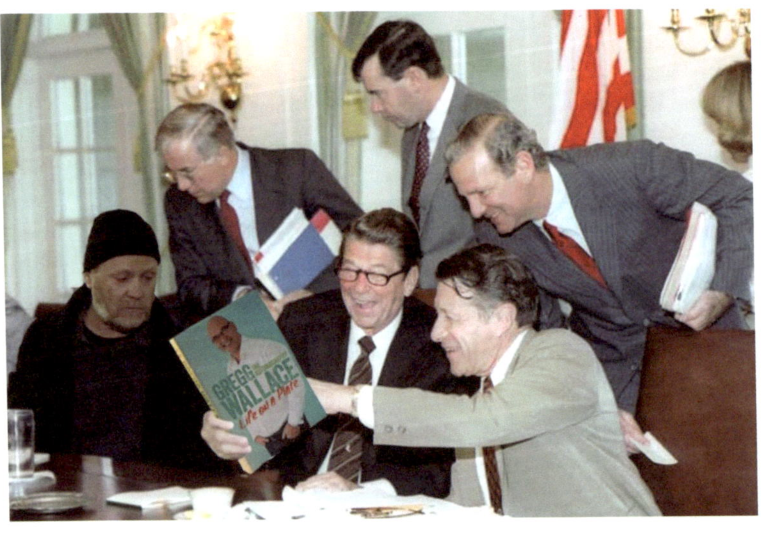
GREGG
WALLACE
Life on a Plate

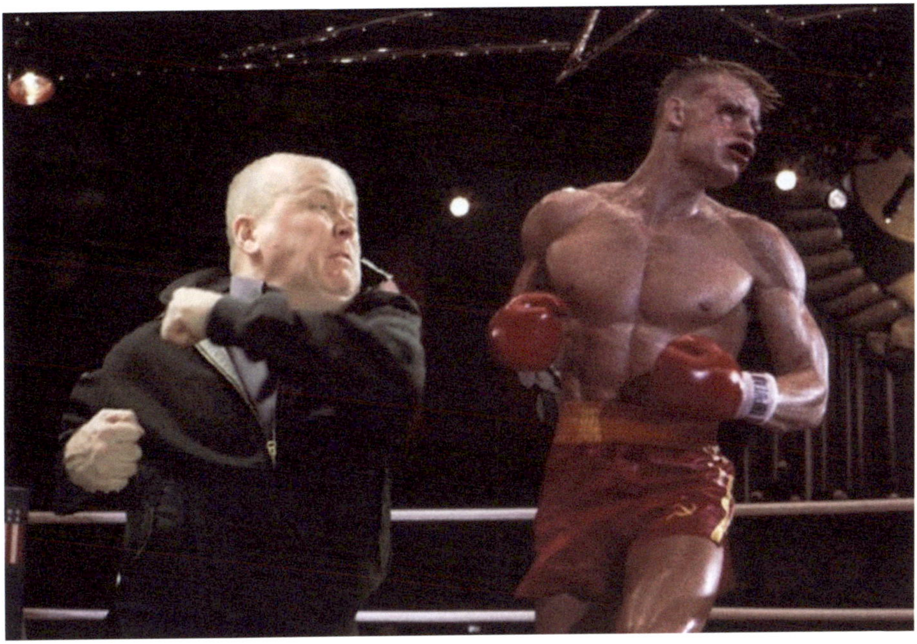

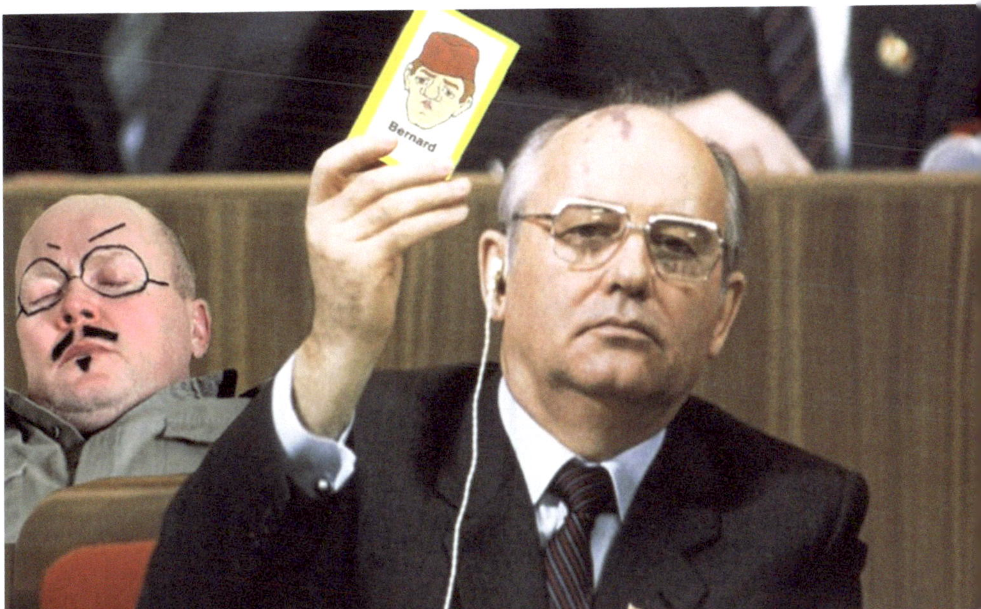

Bernard

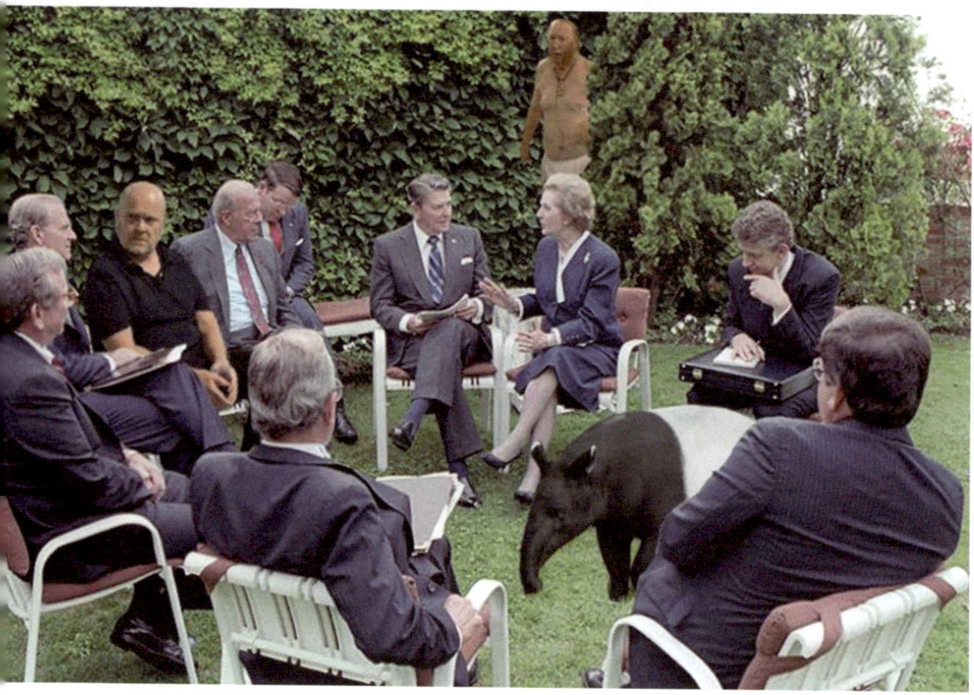

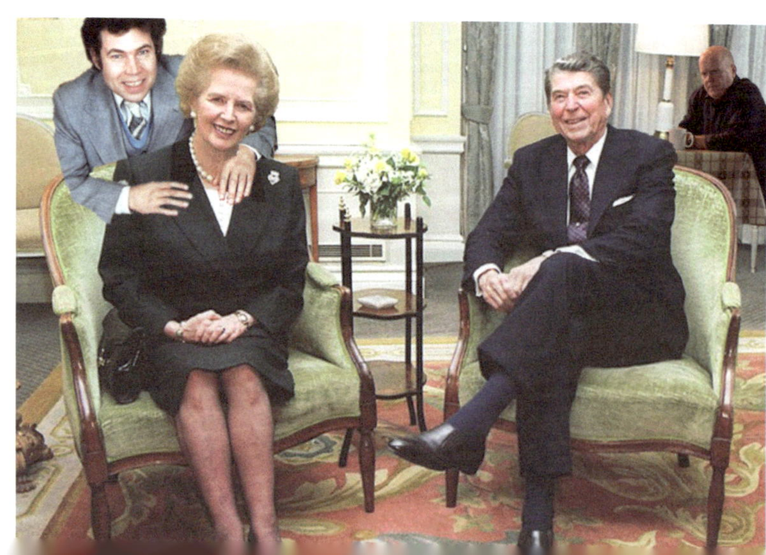

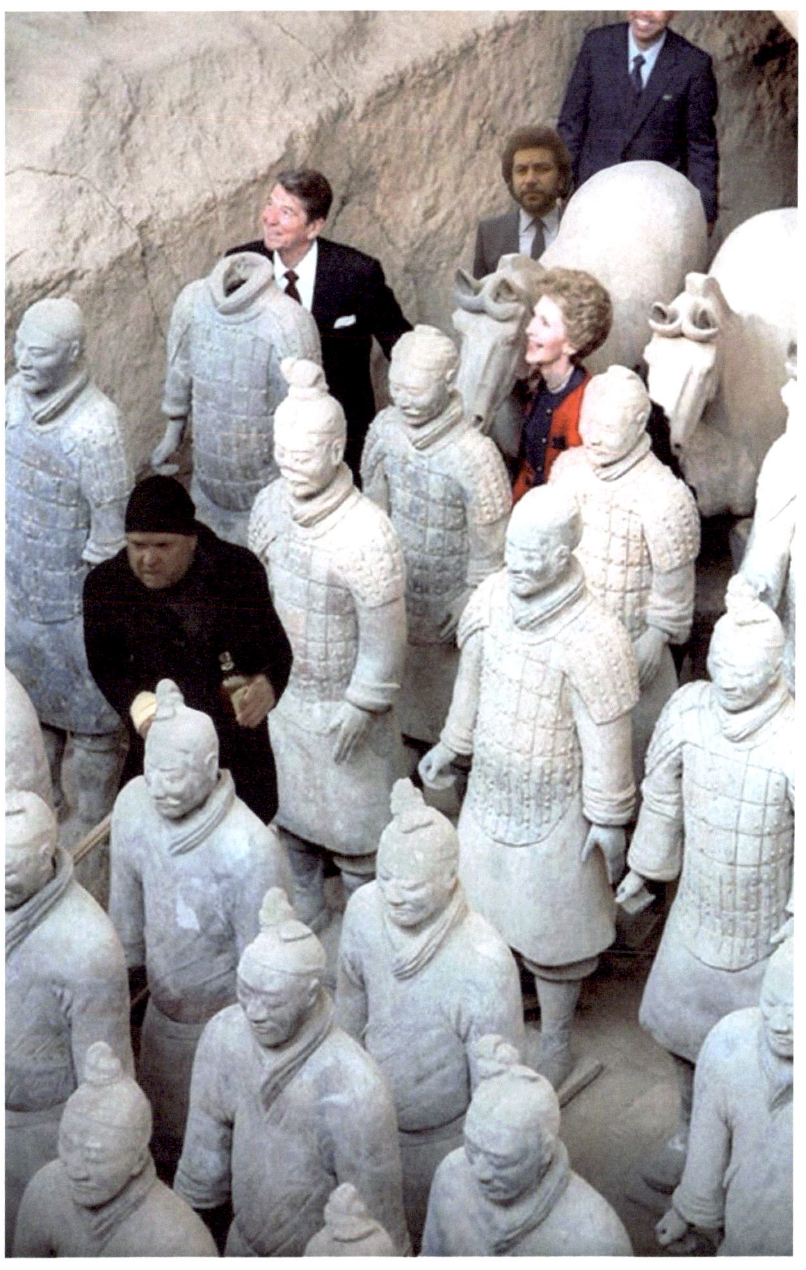

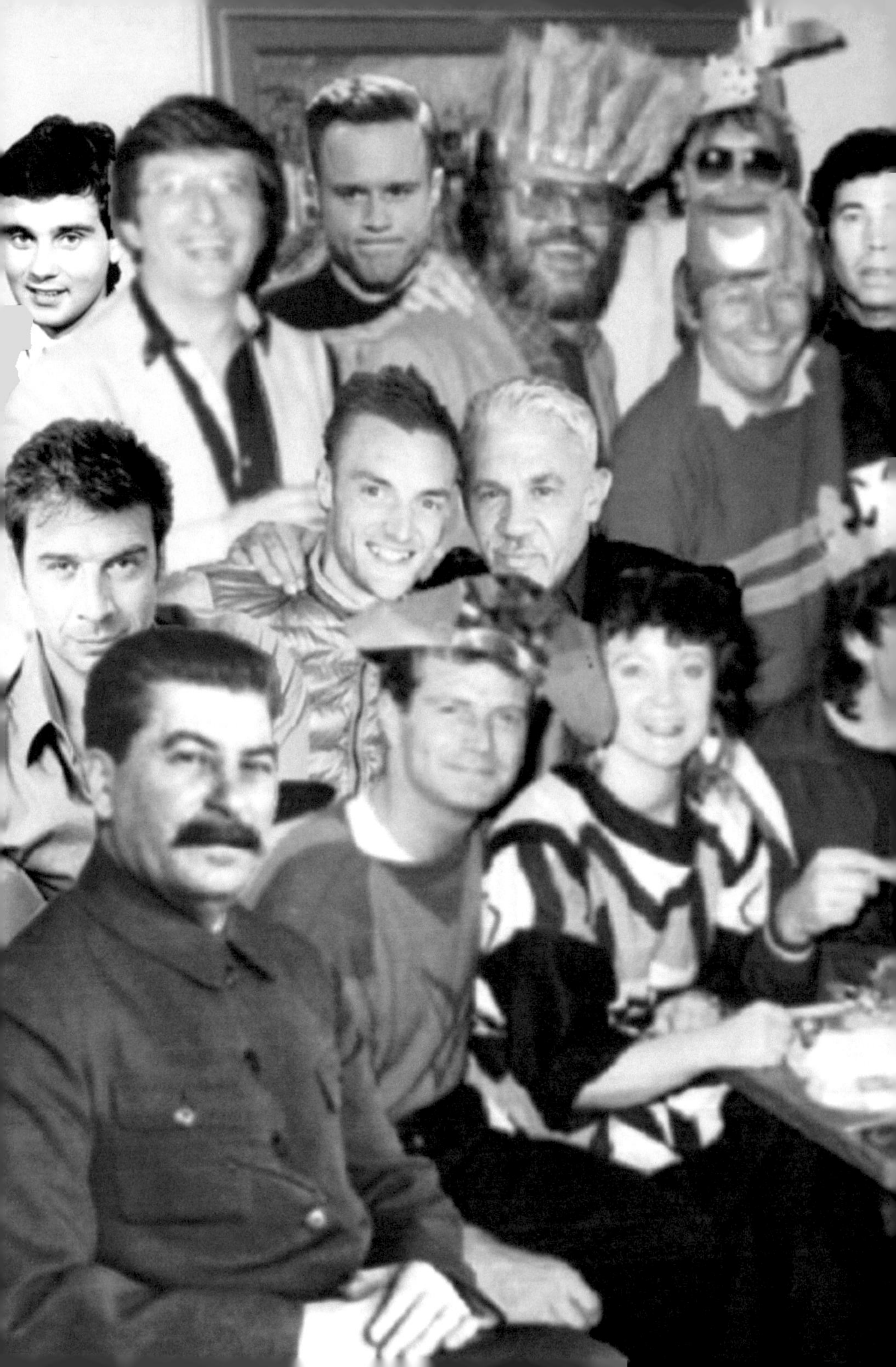

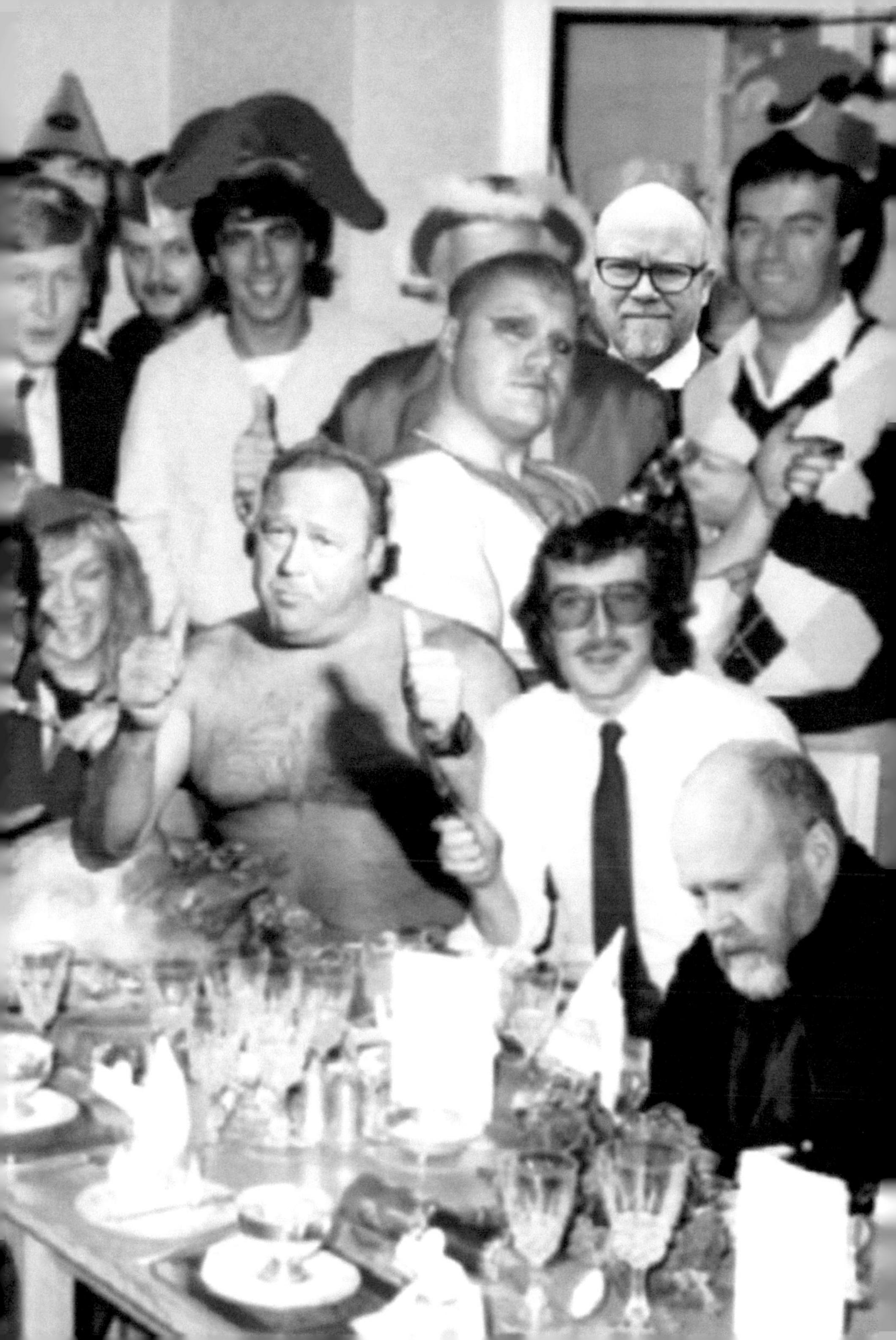

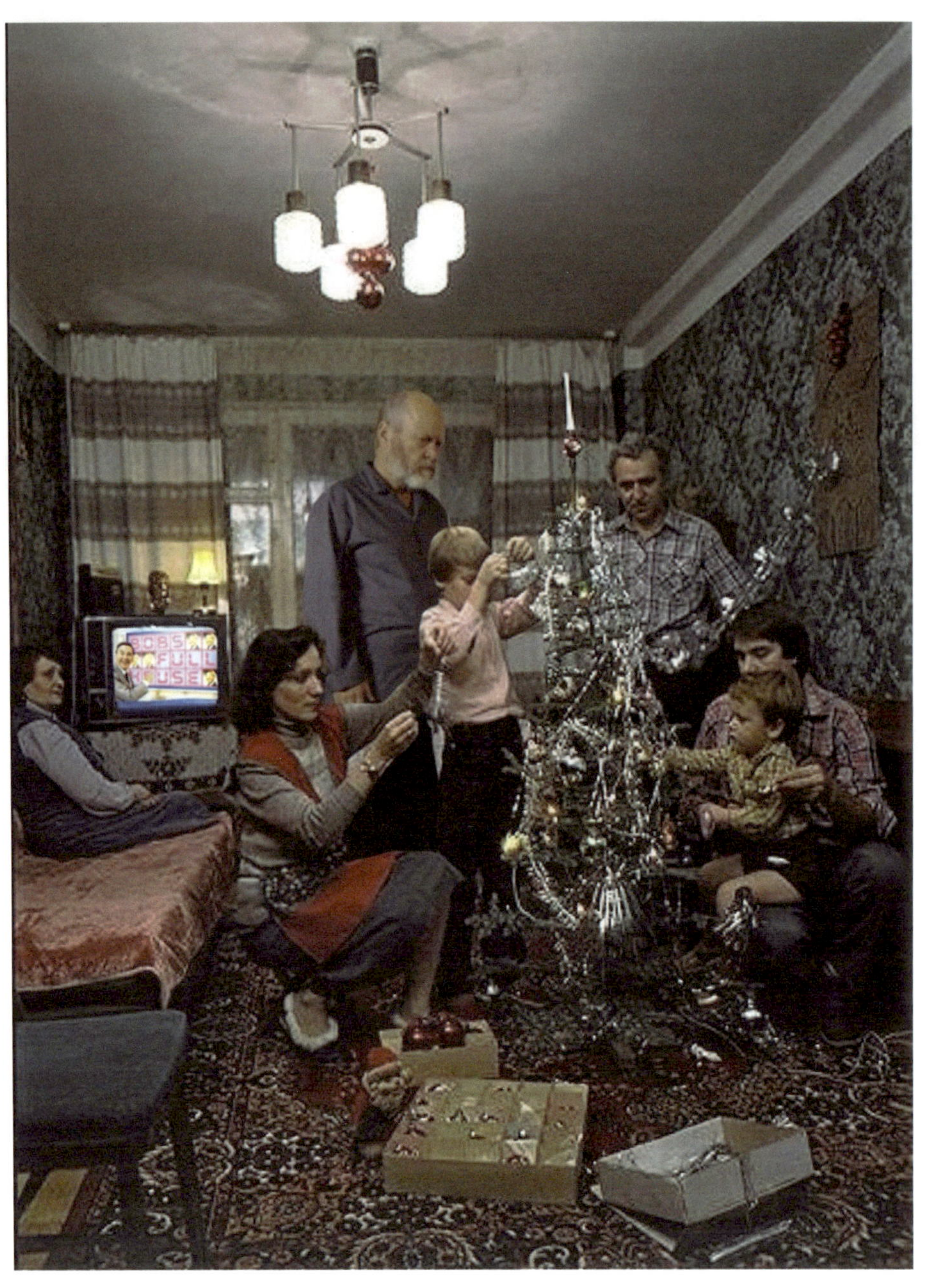
BOBS
FULL